97 WAYS *to* MAKE *a* BABY LAUGH

97 WAYS TO MAKE A BABY LAUGH

by Jack Moore

Photographs *by* Penny Gentieu

WORKMAN PUBLISHING • NEW YORK

Library of Congress Cataloging-in-Publication Data

Moore, Jack

97 ways to make a baby laugh /
written by Jack Moore;
photographs by Penny Gentieu.
p. cm.
ISBN 0-7611-0736-3
1. Infants—Humor.
I. Gentieu, Penny.   II Title.
PN6231 .I5M66 1997
818' .5402—dc21   97-6437 CIP

Workman books are available at special discounts
when purchased in bulk for premiums and sales promotions
as well as for fund-raising or educational use. Special
editions can also be created to specification. For details,
contact the Special Sales Director at the address below.

Workman Publishing Company, Inc.
708 Broadway
New York, NY 10003-9555

Manufactured in the United States of America

10 9 8 7 6 5 4 3

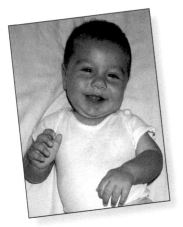

FOR MY SON, BRICK

Acknowledgments

The process of publishing this book began with a one-page letter
to Workman Publishing Company, containing a suggested title and a proposed format.
I was fortunate. Peter Workman took my letter from a giant pile of unsolicited
book proposals and placed it in a much smaller pile while personally responding that
I had a "good concept and title" but he would have to see much more.

Several months later I submitted what I felt was the finished product.
The book was assigned to Ruth Sullivan, my editor, for what I believed were
minor corrections and polishing. Ms. Sullivan did not agree, but rather saw my work
as a skeleton of what the book could and should be. Her candor, suggestions
for changing content and format, and demanding professionalism made this book
so much more than it was in its infancy, and to Ms. Sullivan I am sincerely thankful.

I would also like to extend thanks to my dear friends
Bruce Ender and Laurie Mahan for their assistance, and to the Smith family for their
encouragement and support.

Introduction

BRING A BABY to any grown-up—even the gruffest or most inhibited—and watch what happens. Without exception, they will do something to try and make the baby laugh. Psychologists, anthropologists and other experts have theories about why this is so. For me it's enough to believe that whenever a baby laughs, our humanity is somehow exalted. That is why I wrote this book.

A baby's laughter is infectious and addictive. Once you get that first little giggle, you'll do just about anything to re-create it. But it helps to have a whole repertoire of tricks. Here are 97 very silly, sometimes stupid, but effective ways to make a baby laugh—including sight gags, Laurel & Hardy routines, and parlor tricks. Most are originals developed over several years and tried out on countless babies; some are classics with a unique twist that can make the difference between a smile and a belly laugh. Among the infant-tested formulas are

THE TOP TEN PEEK-A-BOOS, THE GOOGLY FACE CONTEST, THE LIVE JACK-IN-THE-BOX and that old standby, THE RASPBERRY.

I've found that all babies will laugh at some of these skits and some babies will laugh at all of them. It's a matter of taste. Some babies delight in repetition, such as dropping an object from a high chair and having it repeatedly retrieved by Mom or Dad; others relish the unexpected, such as seeing their favorite stuffed animal transported into the room by a remote-control truck. What tickles one baby's funny bone may puzzle or even annoy another.

You will learn by trial and error what works best for your baby. The exercises in this book are geared for babies age three months (when babies first begin to have a sense of humor) to fourteen months (when their increased mobility makes them less than a captive audience). Babies as young as six months begin to appreciate incongruities. In fact, they adore them. Seeing Grandma's glasses on top of her head or the dog wearing a baby bonnet is cause for great hilarity. Or attach that rubber suction toy Baby is used to seeing on his high chair tray to your forehead and you're guaranteed a laugh.

Though the primary purpose of this book was to make babies laugh, a funny and wonderful thing happened along the way. As I experimented by having friends and relatives perform for Baby, even the most reserved would lose their inhibitions and become as goofy as their roles required. When Baby laughed, the show was a smash. But when Baby would give a deadpan reaction, the scene was often even funnier: a roomful of adults laughing hysterically at their failed attempts to make a baby laugh. Performing routines from this little book is a great way to relieve the tension and stress of life with an infant. So lighten up, rediscover your sense of the absurd, and life with Baby will be that much more fun.

1.

THE LIVE JACK-IN-THE-BOX. Put Dad in a large cardboard box. Then have the family sing the familiar tune *Pop Goes the Weasel.* When you get to the last line, Dad jumps out of the box.

2.

THE DISAPPEARING NOODLE. Place the end of a long strand of spaghetti in Dad's mouth and have him suck it in as quickly as possible.

NOTE: *For best results, I prefer cappellini done al dente, but I have friends who swear by linguine.*

3.

THE EXAGGERATED SNEEZE. Fake a sneeze that takes a long time to arrive, as in "Ah-Ah-Ah-Ah-Choo!"

4.

Hold a SILLY FACE CONTEST. Have family members compete for Baby's attention. Whoever gets the biggest laugh is declared the winner.

NOTE: *No props permitted in this one. Here's your chance to take advantage of that walleye, big nose, flexible tongue, wiggling eyebrows or any other fancy trick you've developed through the years.*

5.

Play rap music while Grandma does an improvisational, nonrepetitive break-dance.

NOTE: *Everyone else in the room should clap and repeat the beat, "Go girl! Go girl!"*

6.

With Baby watching, have Mom, Dad or more agile members of the family lift a soccer ball from the floor using nothing but their heads.

EQUIPMENT: *Soccer ball, floor padding*
PHYSICAL MODEL: *Irreproducible*
RISK TO PARENT: *High*
RESULTS: *Inverse ratio of parent's success to success with Baby*

7. THIS LITTLE PIGGY toe play is part of every parent's repertoire. Granted, the original story of pigs going to market is completely lost on Baby, but the line *"Wee Wee Wee all the way home"* rarely fails to bring on peals of laughter.

8. Put on a polka cassette or CD and do a polka with your spouse. (But only if you have absolutely no idea how to actually *do* the polka.) There is something inherently funny about bad polka dancers. Just do it.

9.

PEEK-A-BOO 101. Place your hands over your eyes or over Baby's eyes. Remove hands and say "Pee-ee-k." A favorite version is to have Mom hide her head beneath a blanket and pop out at Baby with a "Boo."

NOTE: *If Baby's response is deadpan, perhaps she's too sophisticated for basic peek-a-boo. See* ADVANCED PEEK-A-BOO, *No. 71.*

10.

THE "SCAMOOCH." This simple laugh-getter originated in Italy and was later revived for adults as "Noogies" on *Saturday Night Live.* Using the knuckles of your index and middle fingers, lightly press against Baby's ribs while jiggling your wrist. Just before doing so, say, *"Somebody's gonna get a Scamooch."*

11.

Clear off a clean surface so there are no other objects to distract Baby. Set up rectangular blocks with just enough space between them for a domino effect. Show Baby how to set off the chain reaction.

NOTE: *Given the setup time versus the payoff for this trick, it might not be a first choice for working moms.*

12.

Another oldie but goodie is BABY'S STINKY FEET. Put your nose close to Baby's feet, and make a face while repeating *"Pee-you, Stinky"* in a high-pitched voice.

NOTE: *"Pee-you, Stinky" gets a laugh consistently. No one knows why.*

13. Blow liquid soap bubbles through a wand for Baby.

NOTE: *For a real giggle, have Dad and Baby's siblings attempt to catch the bubbles on the tips of their noses.*

14.

Have everyone present do a soft-shoe while whistling the tune *Tea for Two*. Please, no substitute tunes.

NOTE: *Trust me on the musical selection. In the history of Hollywood movies and TV, this is the only song ever used for amateur soft-shoeing.*

15.
Fill a trash bag with a couple dozen colored balloons. With Baby watching from a stroller about thirty feet away from the house, release all the balloons at once from a second-story window.

NOTE: *Be sure Baby's head is facing the balloons at release time or you're in for a long afternoon. I learned the hard way.*

16. THE REVERSE BABY MONITOR TRICK.

When Baby is awake, reverse the transmitter and receiver of the sound monitor. Then have familiar voices address Baby from another room just before entering his view.

NOTE: *Our name for this electronic variation on "Peek-a-Boo" is "Hear-a-Boo."*

17. Put a baby cookie in a small bag; put the bag in a small box; put the box in a larger box, and so on. Then have each family member open a box in Baby's view, with Mom opening the final bag and exclaiming "HERE'S Baby's cookie!"

18.

With Baby sitting in the high chair, hold her hands down while you ask, "How big is Baby?" Then, as you raise her arms over her head, add the words "SO BIG."

19.

Keeping your face at a safe distance from Baby, blow a large bubble gum bubble. The slower, the better.

NOTE: *In this trick, timing is everything.*

20.

Make a scented bubble bath for Dad, using three times the amount of soap recommended. Put Dad in the tub so that only his head is exposed above the bubbles. When the stage is set, bring Baby into the room for Show & Smell.

21.

THE RASPBERRY or BRONX CHEER. Moisten your lips, press them lightly against Baby's arm or belly, and blow air out slowly to create a vibrating and tickling sensation. The louder and more impolite the sound, the better.

NOTE: *When all else fails, this old standby almost always gets a rise out of Baby.*

22. THREE-CARD MONTE FOR BABIES.

You've seen the trick where a pea is hidden under one of three walnut shells; the shells are quickly shuffled around and a player is challenged to choose the shell that's hiding the pea. Perform this trick for Baby using three plastic cups and a lemon. Applaud and make a big fuss when Baby finds the hidden lemon.

NOTE: *If there's no reaction, Baby is either too young or doesn't approve of streetside gambling.*

23.

Take a golf ball. Cut a hole in the cover of a shoe box so that the hole is just slightly larger than the ball. Invert the cover and assist Baby in manipulating it until the golf ball falls through the hole.

NOTE: *Every time the ball falls through the hole, say "All gone!" in a surprised but happy voice.*

24. Line up at least four people shoulder to shoulder, facing Baby. Count off 1, 2, 3, etc., starting with the person on the left. Odd-numbered players squat down while even-numbered ones stretch toward the ceiling, saying in high-pitched voices "So high!" Players then switch positions.

NOTE: *This scenario works best with extremely fit performers or especially bright babies.*

25. Put Baby in a stroller or high chair at the foot of a ramp or staircase. Roll a featherweight beach ball down toward Baby, beginning on the first or second step and working your way up. The higher you get, the more Baby laughs.

26. TWO-HEADED HORSEY. Mom and Dad stand back to back, then bend forward from the waist. A sheet draped over their backs creates a one-torso, two-head effect.

NOTE: *Some parents feel compelled to mimic the push-me/pull-me toy when they find themselves in this position.*

27.

Feed Baby from the tip of a large wooden spoon that you pretend is an airplane. Make whatever aerodynamic sounds you can think of as you loop the spoon in large circles in front of Baby. Then gently come in for a "landing" at Baby's lips.

NOTE: *If Baby doesn't open up for the landing, try feeding Mom or Gramps this way.*

28.

BABY BINGO. Distribute Baby's toys to a few family members. Have Mom call out names of toys as the player holding the correct toy yells out "Bingo!" and waves the toy in the air.

NOTE: *"Bingo" is one of the funniest and most underrated words in the English language. Yell it out a few times, and see if you don't agree.*

29.

Stage a "TO-DOO TO-DOO" concert using the cardboard tubes inside a paper towel or toilet tissue roll. For some unknown reason, all children naturally use these tubes as musical instruments. For a "Big Band" effect, recruit the neighbors and Baby, too.

30.

Dad lies on floor, faking sleep and emitting extremely loud, exaggerated snores. Each time Baby touches or pounds on Dad, he sits up in mock surprise.

WARNING: *Since Baby doesn't distinguish between fake and actual sleep, Dad's catnaps are now a thing of the past.*

31. Fill a clean spray bottle with lukewarm water and spray Baby's bare feet.

NOTE: *Some purists consider this cheating. For me, it's a classic.*

32.

Mom holds Baby on her lap facing a fully decorated Christmas tree in a dimly lit room. When she's sure Baby is looking in the right direction, someone lights the tree. This might not sound like a real thriller for you, but it's sure to get a response from Baby.

33.

Dampen a foam rubber or sponge animal so that it can be compressed into a tiny ball that you conceal in the palm of your hand. Turn your palm up and release the toy to its full size in front of Baby.

34.

Make hand puppets by painting faces with nail polish on old white sweat socks. Mom and Dad can put on a four-character show by extending their hands and forearms over the edge of a table so that only the puppets are visible to Baby.

35.

Spice up a solo puppet act with a bit of ventriloquism. For starters, place your tongue on the roof of your mouth against your two front teeth and, without moving your mouth, say "Day-Dee" (that's ventriloquist talk for "Baby"). A mustache helps.

36.

Hold a "Barney" impression contest, with each person introducing himself to Baby with Barney's goofy, hyper-cheerful voice and flipper-like gestures.

NOTE: *If you don't know Barney yet, you will soon.*

37.

Sit down with Baby for a rerun of *The Honeymooners* episode in which Ralph and Ed take mambo lessons. Provide a baby snack for viewing. Have Dad try to duplicate Ralph's exact dance steps for Baby.

38.

With Latin music in the background, form a conga line, and parade past Baby with Mom kicking up her heels in front and Dad bringing up the rear.

39.

Have mother-in-law use a garden hose to spray Dad in his bathing suit.

40.

With music playing in the background, Mom and Dad lie on the floor with feet against feet and do the bicycle exercise. Have someone start and stop the music as a cue to start and stop pedaling.

NOTE: *For the professional touch that Baby commands, rubber-soled shoes are a must.*

41.

THE MAGNET TRICK. You've done it before. Now do it for Baby. Place a metal object, such as a spoon, on Baby's high chair tray. Drag a magnet under the tray so the object appears to move unassisted.

42.

Once Baby can sit up, bounce him on your knee to a song with a surprise ending. A good one is: *Ride away to Boston / Ride away to Lynn / You'd better watch out or / You might fall IN.* On the last line, give a vigorous bounce, open legs and catch Baby as he drops through. After a few repetitions, Baby will start laughing in anticipation of the word "IN."

43.

Paste large pictures of familiar animals on sheets of paper. Players take turns choosing an animal at random, then do a sight and sound imitation of their animal for Baby. Whoever gets the biggest laugh wins.

NOTE: *Extra points if Baby answers back with an animal sound.*

44.

Stage a Hawaiian hula show for Baby. Have the adult males perform in grass skirts and leis while the women sing *Here's to Baby and the Way We Do the Hula-Hoo.*

NOTE: *If grass skirts are unavailable, you may substitute bathing suits, but we cannot guarantee the belly laugh that the real thing elicits.*

45.

Bring Baby to the Laundromat with you and let him watch the tumbling clothes go around in the front-load dryer. Sound boring? Just think back to when you thought that tumbling clothes were quite a sight.

46.

Hang Baby's favorite fluffy toy on a rope suspended from a tree branch, and allow her to push the toy back and forth. Because of the pendulum effect and the absence of friction, Baby's power over the toy is greatly enhanced, and so is her delight.

47.

Set a potted plant or flowers on a phonograph turntable at a safe distance from Baby. Put the turntable on its slowest speed and sing *Ring Around the Rosy* as the plant revolves.

NOTE: *For the benefit of younger parents, a turntable is that thing in the corner of the cellar that Mom and Dad used to play those big plastic records on.*

48.

CHATTERING TEETH AUDITIONS. Place a set of windup teeth on a table. Let them chatter. Then have family members imitate the speed and style of the chattering teeth.

NOTE: *If you don't own chattering teeth, ask around. One of your neighbors surely does.*

49.

Dress Dad and Grandpa in diapers made of sheets or white towels and give each of them a baby bottle. Have them share an afternoon snack with Baby.

NOTE: *Be sure to capture the moment on video or camera. The really hearty laughter will come about twenty years later.*

50.

THE HUMAN CAROUSEL. At a playground, leave Baby with an adult at a safe distance from the merry-go-round. Have family members sit at evenly spaced seats on the carousel, facing outward and waving hello and good-bye to Baby as they pass by again and again.

51.

DINNER & A SHOW. While Baby is eating, have the rest of the family perform at the table by tapping glasses of water with a spoon. Make sure the glasses have different amounts of liquid so they will produce a variety of tones.

NOTE: *Let Baby join in the fun by playing backup percussion with a wooden spoon on his tray.*

52.

LIVING STATUES. Have family dance about the room until Mom touches someone on top of the head, at which point he or she freezes in position. As Mom continues to touch players at random, each one is turned on and off like a windup toy.

NOTE: *Baby will make the connection between movement and Mom's touch much sooner than you would imagine.*

53.
Have Dad sit, facing Baby, with a paper cup balanced upright on his head while his mother-in-law fills the cup from a pitcher. Let Baby see at least a 12-inch stream of water. If Dad is especially level-headed, pour an additional ounce or two.

EQUIPMENT: *Paper cup, pitcher, water*
PREP TIME: *Minimal*
RISK TO PARENT: *Very high*
SUCCESS RATE: *Very high*

54.

MIRROR, MIRROR. Babies adore looking at the most captivating face of all—their own. Hold Baby in your arms so he's facing the mirror, point to his reflection and say, "Look, there's Baby!" Put one hat on you and another on Baby. Switch hats. Then switch them back again.

55.

MECHANICAL SOLDIER. Dad stands as stiff as a toy soldier, with his right arm extended straight out. Mom pushes down the extended arm and Dad automatically raises his other arm, as if mechanically. Repeat. Baby will catch on, and you will get a laugh eventually.

56.

Stage a water pistol fight among all family members in full view of, but at a safe range from Baby. For a multicolor production, use a different food coloring in each of the pistols.

NOTE: *This game is for the truly committed—or the desperate.*

57.

Set Baby in front of the computer and turn on the screensaver. The Flying Toasters, the Lawn Mower and the random moving patterns of Bliss will stimulate and amuse Baby.

NOTE: *If you're techno-nerds, try a non-broadcasting TV station for the black-and-white snow and patterns that used to amuse the flower children of the '60s for hours.*

58.

Punch small holes near the bottom of an empty milk carton. As Baby watches, fill the carton with water to create a shower effect.

NOTE: *The best place to enjoy this is the tub. Hold the carton high to make "rain" on Baby.*

59.

I'M GONNA GET YOU. From about ten feet away, move slowly toward Baby wiggling your fingers and repeating, "I'm gonna GET you," before tickling. Be sure to emphasize the word "get."

60.

Draw a simple cartoon face on a sturdy piece of cardboard. Cut a hole where the mouth would be. When Mom is feeding Baby, have Dad conceal an empty bowl behind the cardboard so that Mom can "feed" the cartoon face in between spoonfuls for Baby.

61.

Have Grandmother squirt whipped cream into Dad's face whenever Baby makes a vocal sound. Continue until Baby laughs or can is empty—whichever comes first.

62.

Wet a small cloth with vanilla extract and allow Baby to smell it. Baby's response will vary from slight smile to laugh, but it's a great forecaster of Baby's future interest in Häagen-Dazs and Ben & Jerry's.

63.

Have several people blow New Year's Eve noisemakers (you know, the kind that expand in and out with your breath) in Baby's direction. Depending on Baby's taste, she might prefer the all-in-unison sound, the left-to-right chain reaction, or the jazzier random-order improv.

64. TREASURE HUNT. Bury Dad in sand up to his neck and seat Baby next to his head. Baby will take it from there.

NOTE: *Remove all potentially dangerous objects from reach, since Baby will naturally amuse himself by taking a few swipes at Dad.*

65.

Put three hats on three people in Baby's view. Then jingle a bell—any bell will do. Each time the bell rings, the players quickly exchange hats, in clockwise order.

NOTE: *My own extensive testing shows that a combination of sombrero, yarmulke and any hat with attached earmuffs works best.*

66. On a large bed, allow Baby to crawl a few feet away from you. Then grab her legs and gently pull her back to her starting position. Most babies will continue their efforts, laughing harder with each repetition.

NOTE: *Some parents objected to this game, saying that it was conditioning Baby to the hopelessness of the human condition. Try not to read too much into these skits—we're just trying to get a laugh.*

67.

Bring Baby in for a ringside seat as Dad sings *a cappella* in his morning shower. Baby is probably the only one who ever has or ever will appreciate Dad's singing.

NOTE: *Babies are totally indiscriminate when it comes to singing. In fact, the more off-key, the better. The more repetitious, the better.*

68.

Have anyone who remembers do his best impression of Al Jolson singing *Rockaby Your Baby with a Dixie Melody.*

NOTE: *For those who have only a passing familiarity with Al Jolson, I promise you, without hesitation, that someone in your extended family does this impression, though he may not be able to get down on his knees.*

69.

I'M GONNA GET YOU, Part II. Dad approaches Baby, saying *"I'm gonna bite you!"* Baby sticks hand in Dad's mouth. Dad bites down softly without fully closing. Baby withdraws hand and laughs victoriously.

70.

A dripping faucet might drive you crazy, but Baby will think it's a hoot. Simply allow your faucet to drip into a half-filled bowl of water within Baby's sight and hearing. Try to adjust the drops to every two or three seconds.

71.

ADVANCED PEEK-A-BOO. Gather several of Baby's favorite people in an adjoining room. Open and close the door, but each time have a different person behind the door say "Boo!" The unexpected changes will delight Baby.

NOTE: *Limit this game to doting relatives. It's not likely to go over big with guests at your Saturday night cocktail party.*

72.

Have Dad feed Baby from a spoon held in the hand of one of his larger dolls or teddy bears.

73.

BABY MAGIC. Tie a string of bright-colored silk kerchiefs end-to-end—the more, the better. Have Dad insert them up his jacket sleeve and let Baby tug the continuous line of silk through Dad's palm.

74.

Tie a shoe to each of the ends of two broomsticks. With the shoes dangling, move the sticks to create a dancing feet effect for Baby. Try a slow shuffle, a tap dance.

NOTE: *Though Baby's booties work just fine, you're apt to get a bigger laugh using Dad's or Granddad's brown wing tips.*

75.

Outside of Baby's view, place a teddy bear on a remote-control truck. (If you don't have one, your neighbor's son does.) Then have the truck transport teddy into and out of Baby's field of vision. With each return trip, sing out "Look who's coming to visit."

76.

Spread confetti over a smooth, flat surface, such as a coffee table. Once you have Baby's attention, vacuum the confetti, using the hose without attachments. Baby will marvel at the disappearing effect.

NOTE: *Reverse the effect by blowing confetti around the room using the vacuum's exhaust vent.*

77.

DOUBLE TAKE. The "double take" is a comic delayed reaction perfected by Dean Martin and Jerry Lewis. Have one person lift a toy into the field of peripheral vision of another while the latter performs his best double take.

NOTE: *Baby will never tire of this sight gag and will develop his own version by the time he's old enough to talk.*

78.

RIDE 'EM COWBOY. Baby watches as Mom rides on the back of Dad, who is crawling on all fours.

NOTE: *Though Baby has never seen a Western, "Gitty-Ups," "Yahoos" and hat-waving by the rider are a must.*

79.

Using a large, clear plastic glass filled with water, blow continuous air bubbles through a straw. All kids, from babies through middle-school children, love this effect and begin imitating it at an early age.

NOTE: *Baby will also enjoy watching you blow bubbles with a straw in his bathwater.*

80.

THE WHITE CLOWN AND ROGUE CLOWN ACT. This was a favorite stock routine in French and Italian circuses. Every time the Rogue Clown bends over to pick up an object, he receives a whack on the rear end from the sophisticated White Clown, which interrupts his effort. Mom and Dad don't need the clown outfits to act this out for Baby.

NOTE: *A giant plastic bat makes the perfect prop, but a straw broom will do.*

81.

Blow up a balloon. Stretch the end of the mouthpiece to allow the air to screech out. Vary the pitch by stretching the mouthpiece to different lengths.

82.

SHADOW PLAY. In a darkened room, shine a flashlight against the wall. Position Baby so that the spontaneous movement of her arms will create shadows. Baby will enjoy the moving patterns even if she doesn't yet connect them to her own body movements.

NOTE: *The only problem you might encounter here will be Dad's or Granddad's insistence on doing "rabbit ears." Avoid this problem by providing them with their own flashlight and wall.*

83.

Turn a fur-lined glove inside out and allow Baby to feel its softness. Then tie a string to the glove, and cause it to move along the floor or table to create a life-like impression. Make meowing or barking sounds depending upon the size of the glove.

NOTE: *Though our fur glove bit got at least a smile from the majority of babies tested, we met a few precocious nine-month-old animal rights activists who want nothing to do with this trick.*

84.

YODELING IN THE CANYON. With Baby on Mom's lap, Dad stands across the room and lets out a resonant "Yodel-ay-he-hoo!" Use the classic Swiss four-repetition method until Baby becomes so familiar with Dad's falsetto voice that the yodel consistently brings a smile.

NOTE: *We've had at least two reports of Dads who went on yodeling for years, causing ostracism from family and neighborhood gatherings.*

85.

TONGUE TEASERS. Stick your tongue out slowly as far as you can —no more than a quarter-inch per second. Pull tongue back at the same speed. Then repeat the motion, this time as quickly as possible. Alternate the methods.

NOTE: *We know you'll do anything to amuse Baby, but we strongly suggest that you NOT practice this technique on buses or subways—or on the job.*

86.

DO A "DANNY." (If Mom and Dad are too young to remember this sight gag from the Danny Thomas show, ask Grandpa to demonstrate.) Take a mouthful of water. Then, acting as if Baby has just made you laugh, turn away and eject the water. With a little practice, you will master the art of emitting a fine, evenly distributed spray with the timing that would make even Danny proud.

87.

SNAKE-IN-THE-GRASS. Stretch a long piece of rope on the ground. Have a person at each end wiggle the rope from side to side so that a series of "waves" are created. Vary the size of the waves to make the snake appear to move faster or slower.

NOTE: *If you've forgotten how to do this, have any kid in the neighborhood demonstrate for Baby. They all know how.*

88. Submerge two different-colored rubber or plastic balls in a tub of water. Release the balls to the surface, one at a time, so that only one ball is ever visible to Baby.

89.

Fill a large laundry bag with Baby's stuffed animals and toys. Bring the bag to Baby and present each toy with great fanfare.

NOTE: *Since Baby cares only about having and holding, not owning, it will be like receiving a new bagful of gifts every time.*

90.

BABY CHANNEL SURFING. Seat Baby in a high chair facing the TV. With close supervision, help Baby press the remote control's channel changer.

NOTE: *In most families, this is the only instance in which Dad will part with his remote.*

91.

FETCH. Now that Baby's here, is Mom missing those aerobic workouts? Place a beach ball on the table surface of Baby's high chair, and stand several feet away. Continue to retrieve and replace the ball until Baby tires of the game or nightfall, whichever comes first (usually the latter).

NOTE: *Mom, if you get bored, think of it this way: your budding Newton is experimenting with cause-and-effect relationships.*

92.

USING YOUR NOGGIN. Attach a suction cup toy—like the one on Baby's high chair tray—to your forehead. Baby will find this trick—and you—a laugh riot.

93.

The oldest trick in the book is probably FUNNY EARS. Insert your thumbs in your ears, with your fingers outstretched and your palms facing Baby; then either wiggle your fingers or use the open-and-close method, whichever gets the bigger laugh.

94.

On a summer day, stage a water balloon toss for Baby. After the balloons have been filled with water and tied, have family and friends form two lines, facing each other, and begin tossing.

95.

At a safe distance from Baby, have Dad illustrate his mastery of the pogo stick.

NOTE: *Depending on Dad's athletic ability, a "safe distance" could range from the width of a driveway to the length of a football field.*

96.

Have Dad play two notes on any musical instrument—a keyboard is best. Play the same two notes over and over as Mom sings *"Bay-bee, Bay-bee"* to the beat. Then reverse, with Mom accompanying Dad in a higher key.

NOTE: *This one will really work; save it for moments of true desperation.*

97. Tie two helium balloons to Grandfather's ears on twelve-inch strings. Dangle two sticks of chewing gum from his upper lips as cartoon-style teeth. Then have Grandpa sing the first few bars of *Be My Love* to Baby in his best Mario Lanza impression.

98.

....

....

....

....

....

....

Insert your own
favorite laugh-getter
and Baby's picture

99.

*Insert your own
favorite laugh-getter
and Baby's picture*

About the Babies

BABIES ARE THE GREATEST AUDIENCE, especially the twenty babies who humored us by sitting for their portraits and laughing at our attempts to make them laugh. So thanks to: Branden, Declan, Hannah, Jack, Janie, Jonathan, Julian, Justin, Kelly, Killian, Liam, Lein, Michael, Nicolas, Orion, River, Ruby, Siobhan, Zachary and Zoe.

About the Author

JACK MOORE is an advertising consultant and comedy writer. Always the children's entertainer and clown at family gatherings, he perfected his ways to make babies laugh when his son, Brick, was born. Friends and family encouraged Jack to write down his "Infant Laugh Formulas" for other parents.

About the Photographer

PENNY GENTIEU is a New York photographer who has specialized in photographing babies and children for the past twelve years. Her photographs are exhibited and published worldwide, and she has to her credit over 100 magazine covers— *Time*, *Newsweek*, *American Baby*, *Baby Talk*, *New York*, *USA Weekend*, *Parents*—and a children's book *Wow Babies!*